Level 3

Re-told by: Mo Sanders
Series Editor: Rachel Wilson

Pearson Education Limited
KAO Two
KAO Park, Harlow,
Essex, CMI7 9NA, England
and Associated Companies throughout the world.

ISBN: 978-1-2923-4677-9

This edition first published by Pearson Education Ltd 2020

9 10 8

Heinemann Roman Special, 14pt/23pt
Printed by Neografia, Slovakia

Published by Pearson Education Limited

Acknowledgments
Alamy Stock Photo: Jan Wlodarczyk 23, Pictorial Press Ltd 27, Vintage Images 27
Getty Images: firina 24, FPG / Staff/ Moviepix 26, Image Source 22, Kristen Prahl 24
Shutterstock.com: optimarc 27, Pixel-Shot 22, Purino 22, stockfotoart 22

For a complete list of the titles available in the Pearson English Readers series, visit
www.pearsonenglishreaders.com.

Alternatively, write to your local Pearson Education office or
to Pearson English Readers Marketing Department,
Pearson Education, KAO Two, KAO Park, Harlow, Essex, CMI7 9NA

In This Book

Andy

A boy with some great toys

Woody

A toy sheriff and Andy's favorite toy

Buzz Lightyear

A cool toy and Woody's friend

Al

A man with a big toy store

Jessie and Bullseye

A cowgirl doll and her horse

Stinky Pete

A toy from Woody's TV show

Before You Read

Introduction

A man takes Woody because he wants to sell him for a lot of money. Buzz and all of Andy's toys want to find their friend and bring him home. But where is Woody? And does he want to come home?

. . . .

Activities

1 **Look at the pictures in the story and choose the right answers.**

1 On page 2, what does Al want to do?

   a buy the toy   **b** take the toy   **c** sell the toy

2 On page 4, what does Woody want to do?

   a leave   **b** be on TV   **c** go to a museum

3 On page 12, what does Buzz want to do?

   a bring his friend home   **b** go to the airport   **c** meet new toys

2 **Match the words to the sentences. You can use a dictionary.**

apartment   museum   conveyor belt   yard sale

1 This moves bags at an airport.

2 You can live in one of these.

3 You can go and see old things in this place.

4 People can buy things at one of these.

Andy played with his toys for one last time before summer camp.
But Woody's arm ripped. Andy was sad because Woody was his
favorite toy. "Now I can't take Woody to camp!" he said.

The next day, Andy's mom wanted to have a yard sale.
She looked for old toys in Andy's room and carried them
outside in a box.
Andy's toys watched the yard sale from the window.
Oh, no! Woody was in the box.

There was a man by the table. Andy's
mom looked away and the man moved fast.
"He's taking Woody!" Buzz cried.
The man carried Woody to his car.

A little later, Woody was in the man's apartment at the top of a tall building. The man put Woody in a glass case. Woody was afraid. He wanted to go home.

Suddenly, a cowgirl doll cried, "Woody, it's you!"
Her name was Jessie. There was also a horse, and an old man
doll in his box. His name was Stinky Pete.
"How do you know my name?" Woody asked Jessie.

Jessie showed him. Woody was a famous toy! There was an old TV show about him. Jessie, Stinky Pete, and Bullseye were also in the show.

Woody was surprised, but it was nice to be famous.

"Now we can go to the museum!" Stinky Pete cried.

"What museum?" Woody asked.

"Al wants to sell us to a museum in Japan," Stinky Pete said.

"I can't go to Japan!" Woody cried. "I have to go home."

Jessie was sad and angry. "Jessie's sad because the museum has to have *all* of us," Stinky Pete said. "We can only go *with you*." Woody didn't know what to do. Perhaps it was better to go?

In Andy's room, the toys watched a TV commercial for
Al's Toy Store. Al was the man from the yard sale! And there
was an address!

"I have to go," Buzz said.

"You can't go, Buzz. It's dangerous!" Rex cried.

"I have to get Woody," Buzz said.

The toys wanted to bring their friend home.

First, some of them climbed out of the bedroom window.

Then, they walked a long way. The roads were very dangerous and they started to get tired.

Suddenly, there was Al's car outside an apartment building. Al walked through the doors. It was his apartment building. But was Woody inside? Buzz started to run across the road.

The toys climbed through the building's air vents and arrived at Al's apartment.

"Woody, you're okay!" Buzz cried. "We have to leave now."

"Al is selling you to a toy museum in Japan," Rex said quickly.

"I want to go to Japan," Woody said. "Andy doesn't want me."

Buzz and the toys were surprised. Sadly, they turned
to leave.

Then Woody listened to a song about friends on the Woody
TV show. Suddenly, he jumped up.

"Buzz, wait! I'm coming with you!" he shouted.

Then Woody said to his new friends, "Come with me! You can also be Andy's toys. You can make a child happy."
Jessie and Bullseye were excited but Stinky Pete was angry. He jumped in front of them. "No way! We have to go to the museum!" he shouted.

Suddenly, the door opened. Al was back in the apartment. He started to put Woody, Jessie, Stinky Pete, and Bullseye into his case. He was ready to take them to the airport. It was time to go to Japan.

Buzz and his friends were outside now. They watched Al leave the
building with Woody in his green case. Al started to drive away.
"How can we get Woody now?" Rex cried.

The answer was easy. There was a truck next to the road!
The toys jumped in and Buzz started to drive. They followed
Al's car all the way to the airport.

At the airport, Al was at the ticket desk. He put the case on the conveyor belt for the plane.

"Let's go!" Buzz cried. The toys jumped into a pet box and moved on to the conveyor belt.

There were a lot of cases on the conveyor belt. Which was the right one?

There it was! Buzz started to run.

Buzz opened Al's case and Woody, Jessie, and Bullseye jumped out.

"Goodbye, Stinky Pete!" Woody cried. "Let's go home."

Andy arrived home from summer camp. His toys were there
to welcome him. And there were some new ones.

"Oh, wow! New toys. Cool!" Andy cried.

Jessie and Bullseye were happy—they were Andy's toys now.

After You Read

1 Match the names to the sentences.

Woody   Al   Jessie   Stinky Pete   Buzz

1 He wants to help his friend.
2 She wants Woody to stay.
3 There was an old TV show about him.
4 He wants to go to the museum in Japan.
5 He wants to sell the toys.

2 Put the story into the correct order.

a Buzz opens the case at the airport.
b Woody meets Jessie and Stinky Pete.
c Woody's arm rips.
d Buzz and the toys try to take Woody home.
e A man takes Woody away.

3 Look at the pictures in the story and answer the questions.

1 Why is Andy sad? (page 1)
2 Why is Woody surprised? (page 4)
3 Why is Stinky Pete angry? (page 14)
4 Why is Jessie happy? (page 20)

Picture Dictionary

address

air vent

apartment

camp

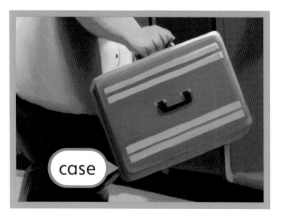

case

climb

conveyor belt

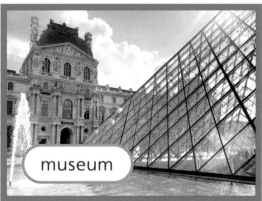

museum

rip

famous

TV show

yard sale

Phonics

Say the sounds. Read the words.

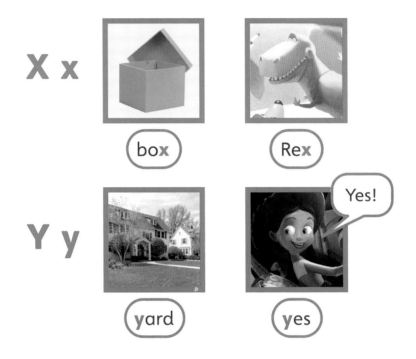

X x

box

Rex

Y y

Yes!

yard

yes

Say the rhyme.

Is Rex in the box for the yard sale today?

No, he's here and he wants to play.

Is the sheriff in the box for the yard sale today?

Yes, and a man is taking him away!

Values

Be a good friend.

Now we can go home!

What about Bullseye and me? We aren't Andy's toys.

And there are a lot of new friends for you to meet.

You are now! Come live with us.

Thanks, Woody! Thanks, Buzz

Find Out

Why did people move to the American West?

In the 1800s, many Americans wanted to find a new life in the country's West. Many people used wagons and horses to get there. They lived and worked on small farms. It was a difficult life.

wagon

- ...ome people were excited to go to California.
  In ...was gold there! People looked for it in the rivers
  ...under the ground.

...n some places in the West, there were big farms
called ranches, with a lot of cows. Cowboys and
cowgirls worked on those ranches.

gold

There was gold in this river!

cowboy